about the author

Robert Fisher is a lecturer and well-known editor of children's poetry anthologies. He has published four previous volumes with Faber and Faber: *Amazing Monsters* and *Ghosts Galore* (both illustrated by Rowena Allen), *Funny Folk* (illustrated by Penny Dann) and *Pet Poems* (illustrated by Sally Kindberg). In addition he has published eight books for teachers. He is married, has two sons and lives in Kew.

also edited by Robert Fisher

AMAZING MONSTERS
Verses to Thrill and Chill

GHOSTS GALORE
Haunting Verse

FUNNY FOLK
Poems about People

PET POEMS

WITCH WORDS

Poems of
Magic and Mystery

edited by
Robert Fisher

illustrated by
Shirley Felts

faber and faber
LONDON · BOSTON

First published in Great Britain in 1987
by Faber and Faber Limited
3 Queen Square London WC1N 3AU

This paperback edition first published in 1991

Photoset by Wilmaset, Birkenhead, Wirral
Printed in Great Britain by
Clays Ltd, St Ives plc

A CIP record for this book
is available from the British Library.

ISBN 0–571–16139–X

Contents

Acknowledgements

The editor is grateful for permission to use the following copyright
material:

'Charming' from *The Soul is the Breath in the Body* by Jeni Couzyn.
© 1970 Jeni Couzyn. Reprinted by kind permission of Curtis Brown
on behalf of the author.

'Spell to Banish Fear' by Jeni Couzyn, by permission of the author.

'Maggia' by Janice Cudmore, from *Mirror Poems* published by Ginn
and Company Ltd.

'The Witch' by Walter de la Mare, by permission of the Literary
Trustees of Walter de la Mare and The Society of Authors as their
representative.

'Let Us In' by Olive Dove, by permission of the author.

'W is for Witch' from *The Children's Bells* and 'The Witch! The Witch!'
from *Silver Sand and Snow*, both by Eleanor Farjeon, published by
Michael Joseph.

'The Two Witches' from *Collected Poems 1975* by Robert Graves, by
permission of the Executors of the Estate of Robert Graves.

'A Moon-witch' from *Moon Bells* by Ted Hughes, published by Chatto
and Windus, reprinted by permission of Faber and Faber Ltd.

'The Wood Witch' by Norah Hussey, from *Poems for Movement*
published by Bell & Hyman.

'Hallowe'en' by John Kitching, from *A Second Poetry Book*, published
by the Oxford University Press, 1980, reprinted by permission of
the author.

'Hallowe'en' by Marie A. Lawson, from *Child Life Magazine*, © 1936,
1964 by Rand McNally & Company.

'Green Magic' from *Green Magic* by Edward Lowbury, by permission
of the author.

'Witch Nastee Spella's Hallowe'en Stew' and 'Witch Nastee Spella's
Arrival in Hangman's Wood' by Wes Magee, by permission of the
author.

'Recipe' and 'Frogday' from *Smile Please, Witches* by Shelagh McGee,
published by Robson Books Ltd.

'One Wild Witch' by Judith Nicholls, by permission of the author.

'Witch's Cat' from *Midnight Forest* by Judith Nicholls, reprinted by
permission of Faber and Faber Ltd.

'Space Traveller' by James Nimmo, reprinted by permission of the author.

'The Alchemist' from *Song of the City* by Gareth Owen, published by Fontana Paperbacks.

'The Spell of a Witch' by Gillian Parker, from Cadbury's *First Book of Children's Poetry*, © Cadbury Ltd.

'Spell of Creation' from *Collected Poems* by Kathleen Raine, published by Allen & Unwin.

'Spells' from *James Reeves: The Complete Poems*, © James Reeves Estate. Reprinted by permission of the James Reeves Estate.

'Mixed Brews' and 'The Witchs' Call' from *The Golden Unicorn* by Clive Sansom, published by Methuen.

'Riddle' and 'Spell' by Ian Serraillier, © 1973, 1976 Ian Serraillier, in *I'll Tell You a Tale*, Longman Group and Puffin Books.

'The Witch's Cat' by Ian Serraillier, © 1963 Ian Serraillier, in *Happily Ever After*, Oxford University Press.

'The Turn of the Road' by James Stephens, by permission of The Society of Authors on behalf of the copyright owner, Mrs Iris Wise.

'Hallowe'en: A Poem for Bedtime' by Alan Temperley, reprinted by permission of the author.

'The Witch's Work Song' from *The Sword in the Stone* by T. H. White, published by William Collins, Sons and Co. Ltd.

'Beware' by Joe Wood from *Festive Occasions in the Primary School*, published by Ward Lock, reprinted by permission of the author.

From witches and wizards and longtail'd buzzards,
And creeping things that run in hedge bottoms,
Good Lord deliver us.

Witch Words

What were those words
I caught in the wind
as it sighed and shuffled
all soft and muffled
like a will-o'-the-wisp
wisp wisp-whispering
which words? which words?

Words like seeds scatter in the air
grow in the mind
or wither and die
blurred and unheard
like the wind
wisp wisp-whispering
which words? which words?

These words have flown from crooked lips
the rain spits
the air is alive
these words are flying, seeking, crying,
these words are sighing, fleeting, dying,
words that were caught in the wind
wisp wisp-whispering
which words? WITCH WORDS!

Robert Fisher

Meet-on-the-Road

'Now, pray, where are you going?' said Meet-on-the-Road.
'To school, sir, to school, sir,' said Child-as-it-Stood.

'What have you in your basket, child?' said Meet-on-the-Road.
'My dinner, sir, my dinner, sir,' said Child-as-it-Stood.

'What have you for dinner, child?' said Meet-on-the-Road.
'Some pudding, sir, some pudding, sir,' said Child-as-it-Stood.

'Oh, then, I pray, give me a share,' said Meet-on-the-Road.
'I've little enough for myself, sir,' said Child-as-it-Stood.

'What have you got that cloak on for?' said Meet-on-the-Road.
'To keep the wind and cold from me,' said Child-as-it-Stood.

'I wish the wind would blow through you,' said Meet-on-the-Road.
'Oh, what a wish! What a wish!' said Child-as-it-Stood.

'Pray, what are those bells ringing for?' said
  Meet-on-the Road.
'To ring bad spirits home again,' said Child-as-
  it-Stood.

'Oh, then I must be going, child!' said Meet-
  on-the-Road.
'So fare you well, so fare you well,' said Child-
  as-it-Stood.

Anon

Hinx, Minx, the Old Witch Winks

Hinx, minx, the old witch winks,
The fat begins to fry.
Nobody at home but jumping Joan,
Father, mother and I.
Stick, stock, stone dead,
Blind man can't see;
Every knave will have a slave,
You and I must be he.

Anon

A Charm for Travellers

Here I am and forth I must:
In Jesus Christ is all my trust.
No wicked thing do me no spite,
Here nor elsewhere, day nor night.
The Holy Ghost and the Trinity
Come betwixt my evil spirit and me.

Anon

Charm to Cure Cramp

The Devil is tying a knot in my leg,
Matthew, Mark, Luke and John, unloose it I beg:
Crosses three we make to ease us,
Two for the thieves and one for Christ Jesus.

Anon

The Witch from Rodmell

I once met a witch from Rodmell,
Who screamed like a bat out of hell.
    She jumped on to her broom,
    And flew out of the room –
I only asked her how to spell!

Anon

Hay-ho for Hallowe'en!

Hay-ho for Hallowe'en!
And the witches to be seen,
Some black, and some green,
Hay-ho for Hallowe'en!

Anon

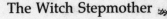

The Witch Stepmother

'I was but seven year old
   When my mother she did die;
My father married the very worst woman
   The world did ever see.

'For she has made me the loathly worm
   That lies at the foot of the tree,
And my sister Maisry she's made
   The mackerel of the sea.

'And every Saturday at noon
   The mackerel comes to me,
And she takes my loathly head
   And lays it on her knee,
She combs it with a silver comb,
   And washes it in the sea.

'Seven knights have I slain,
   Since I lay at the foot of the tree,
And were you not my own father,
   The eighth one you should be.'

The father sent for his lady,
   As fast as send could he:
'Where is my son that you sent from me,
   And my daughter Lady Maisry?'

'Your son is at our king's court,
   Serving for meat and fee;
And your daughter's at our
     queen's court,
   A waiting-woman is she.'

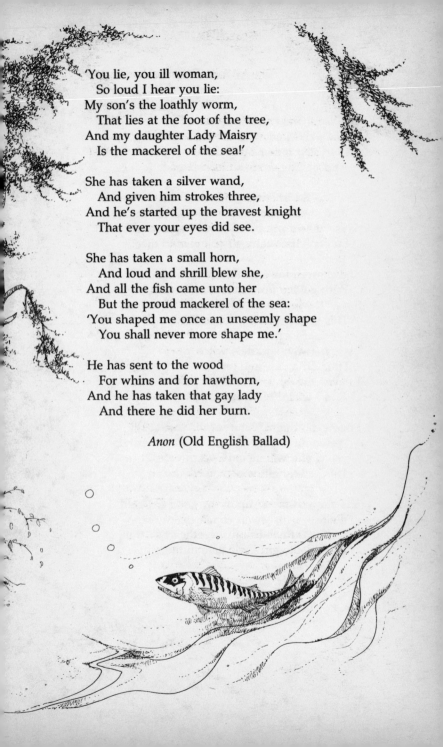

'You lie, you ill woman,
    So loud I hear you lie:
My son's the loathly worm,
    That lies at the foot of the tree,
And my daughter Lady Maisry
    Is the mackerel of the sea!'

She has taken a silver wand,
    And given him strokes three,
And he's started up the bravest knight
    That ever your eyes did see.

She has taken a small horn,
    And loud and shrill blew she,
And all the fish came unto her
    But the proud mackerel of the sea:
'You shaped me once an unseemly shape
    You shall never more shape me.'

He has sent to the wood
    For whins and for hawthorn,
And he has taken that gay lady
    And there he did her burn.

Anon (Old English Ballad)

Alison Gross

O Alison Gross that lives in yon tower,
  The ugliest witch in the north country,
Has trysted me one day up to her bower,
  And many fair speeches she made to me.

She stroked my head and she combed my hair,
  And she set me down softly on her knee;
Says, 'If you will be my sweetheart so true,
  So many fine things I will give to thee.'

She showed me a mantle of red scarlet,
  With golden flowers and fringes fine;
Says, 'If you will be my sweetheart so true,
  This goodly gift it shall be thine.'

'Away, away, you ugly witch,
  Hold far away, and let me be!
I never will be your sweetheart so true,
  And I wish I were out of your company.'

She next brought a shirt of the softest silk,
  Well wrought with pearls about the band;
Says, 'If you will be my sweetheart so true,
  This goodly gift you shall command.'

She showed me a cup of the good red gold,
  Well set with jewels so fair to see;
Says, 'If you will be my sweetheart so true,
  This goodly gift I will give to thee.'

'Away, away, you ugly witch,
  Hold far away, and let me be!
I would not once kiss your ugly mouth
  For all the gold in the north country.'

She's turned her right and round about,
  And thrice she blew on a grass-green horn;
And she swore by the moon and the stars above
  That she'd make me rue the day I was born.

Then out she has taken a silver wand,
  And she's turned her three times round and round;
She muttered such words that my strength it failed
  And I fell down senseless on the ground.

She's turned me into an ugly worm,
  And made me toddle about the tree;
And aye, on every Saturday night,
  My sister Maisry came to me,

With silver basin and silver comb,
  To comb my headie upon her knee;
But before I'd have kissed with Alison Gross,
  I'd sooner have toddled about the tree.

But as it fell out, on last Hallowe'en,
  When the Fairy Court came riding by,
The Queen lighted down on a flowery bank,
  Not far from the tree where I used to lie.

She took me up in her milk-white hand,
  And she's stroked me three times over her knee;
She changed me again to my own proper shape,
  And no more I toddle about the tree.

Anon (Old English Ballad)

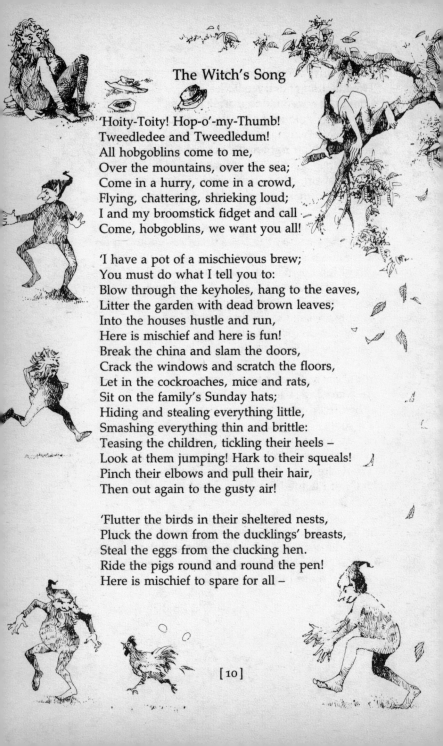

The Witch's Song

'Hoity-Toity! Hop-o'-my-Thumb!
Tweedledee and Tweedledum!
All hobgoblins come to me,
Over the mountains, over the sea;
Come in a hurry, come in a crowd,
Flying, chattering, shrieking loud;
I and my broomstick fidget and call
Come, hobgoblins, we want you all!

'I have a pot of a mischievous brew;
You must do what I tell you to:
Blow through the keyholes, hang to the eaves,
Litter the garden with dead brown leaves;
Into the houses hustle and run,
Here is mischief and here is fun!
Break the china and slam the doors,
Crack the windows and scratch the floors,
Let in the cockroaches, mice and rats,
Sit on the family's Sunday hats;
Hiding and stealing everything little,
Smashing everything thin and brittle:
Teasing the children, tickling their heels –
Look at them jumping! Hark to their squeals!
Pinch their elbows and pull their hair,
Then out again to the gusty air!

'Flutter the birds in their sheltered nests,
Pluck the down from the ducklings' breasts,
Steal the eggs from the clucking hen.
Ride the pigs round and round the pen!
Here is mischief to spare for all –

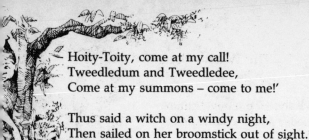

Hoity-Toity, come at my call!
Tweedledum and Tweedledee,
Come at my summons – come to me!'

Thus said a witch on a windy night,
Then sailed on her broomstick out of sight.

Ruth Bedford

The Witch's House

Its wicked little windows leer
   Beneath a mouldy thatch,
And village children come and peer
   Before they lift the latch.

A one-eyed crow hops to the door,
   Fat spiders crowd the pane,
And dark herbs scattered on the floor
   Waft fragrance down the lane.

It sits so low, the little hutch,
   So secret, shy and squat,
As if in its mysterious clutch
   It nursed one knew not what

That beggars passing by the ditch
   Are haunted with desire
To force the door, and see the witch
Vanish in flames of fire.

Laura Benét

Charming

You can sell them for a penny to
your mother

or

You can tie knots for each one
in a piece of string
and plant it at the bottom of your garden
and water it
every morning
that makes them grow under the earth

or

You can have them charmed
if you know a charmer
there are lots in Cornwall you must
leave her a gift and not say thank you
then she will sing
an incantation

or

there is the witch's way.
You take a special white round stone
for every one
and put them in a pretty red bag
into the middle of the road –

Don't touch that bag it's got
warts in it

or

If you can find the green toad you
got them from you can
give them back to him if he'll have them

                                                                    or

You can rub snails on them or slugs
and if that doesn't cure them

you still want them.

Jeni Couzyn

Spell to Banish Fear

By the warmth of the sun
By the baby's cry
By the lambs on the hill
I banish thee.

By the sweetness of the song
By the warm rain falling
By the hum of grass
Begone.

Jeni Couzyn

The Witch

I have walked a great while over the snow,
And I am not tall nor strong.
My clothes are wet, and my teeth are set,
And the way was hard and long.
I have wandered over the fruitful earth,
But I never came here before.
Oh, lift me over the threshold, and let me in at the
                                        door!

The cutting wind is a cruel foe.
I dare not stand in the blast.
My hands are stone, and my voice a groan,
And the worst of death is past.
I am but a little maiden still,
My little white feet are sore.
Oh, lift me over the threshold, and let me in at the
                                        door!

Her voice was the voice that women have,
Who plead for their heart's desire.
She came – she came – and the quivering flame
Sank and died in the fire.
It never was lit again on my hearth
Since I hurried across the floor,
To lift her over the threshold, and let her in at the
                                        door.

Mary Coleridge

The Witch

Weary went the old Witch,
Weary of her pack,
She sat her down by the churchyard wall,
And jerked it off her back.

The cord brake, yes, the cord brake,
Just where the dead did lie,
And Charms and Spells and Sorceries
Spilled out beneath the sky.

Weary was the old Witch;
She rested her old eyes
From the lantern-fruited yew trees,
And the scarlet of the skies;

And out the dead came stumbling,
From every rift and crack,
Silent as moss, and plundered
The gaping pack.

They wish them, three times over,
Away they skip full soon:
Bat and Mole and Leveret,
Under the rising moon;

Owl and Newt and Nightjar:
They take their shapes and creep
Silent as churchyard lichen,
While she squats asleep.

All of these dead were stirring,
Each unto each did call,
'A Witch, a Witch is sleeping
Under the churchyard wall;

'A Witch, a Witch is sleeping . . .'
The shrillness ebbed away;
And up the way-worn moon clomb bright,
Hard on the track of day.

She shone, high, wan, and silvery;
Day's colours paled and died:
And, save the mute and creeping worm,
Nought else was there beside.

Names may be writ; and mounds rise;
Purporting, Here be bones:
But empty is that churchyard
Of all save stones.

Owl and Newt and Nightjar,
Leveret, Bat, and Mole
Haunt and call in the twilight
Where she slept, poor soul.

Walter de la Mare

W is for Witch

I met a wizened woman
As I walked on the heath,
She had an old black bonnet
Her small eyes peeped beneath,
Her garments were so shabby
She couldn't have been rich,
She hobbled with a crutchstick,
And I knew she was a Witch.

She peered at me so slyly
It made my heart feel queer,
She mumbled as she passed me,
But what I couldn't hear.
I smiled at her for answer
And wished her a good day,
She nodded and she chuckled
And she hobbled on her way.

And so I got home safely.
I didn't drop the eggs,
My nose had grown no longer,
My legs were still my legs,
I didn't lose my penny
Or tumble in a ditch –
So mind you smile and say 'Good Day'
When *you* meet a Witch.

Eleanor Farjeon

The Witch! The Witch!

The Witch! the Witch! don't let her get you!
Or your Aunt wouldn't know you the next time she met you!

Eleanor Farjeon

Hallowe'en Fright

Who goes there
stopping at my door
in the deep dark dead
of the moonless night?

Who goes there
turning the handle of my door
without a creak or rattle
slowly
round and round?

Who goes there
through the open-crack door
sliding
without a sound
across the carpeted floor?

Who goes there
with its shadow on the wall
passing with a sigh
and a shiver
through the mirror?

Who goes there
moving by the curtain
coming always closer
silent as a shimmer in the silvery light?

Who goes there
in the clothing of a dream
in the breath of fear
with no noise
ever near ever near
who goes . . .
                    HERE!

Robert Fisher

I'm Coming . . .

(Song of a mean witch, sung in the dark)

I'm coming . . .
   to guzzle your gizzards
     and knobble your knees
   to mingle your innards
     and jam your barees

I'm coming . . .
   to whiffle your waffle
     and bully your beans
   to sniffle your snoffle
     and grobble your greens

I'm coming . . .
   to splatter your mallocks
     and grind your grooves
   to gollop your grollocks
     and splay your trooves

I'm coming . . .
   to stick a newt down your chute
     and a cock in your snooks
   to put a root in your hoot
     and to stick up your dukes

I'm coming . . .
   to bungle your brains
     and hull your baloo
   to wrack you in pains
     and doodle you too

Who's coming . . .
               to who?

I'M COMING . . .
              to YOU!

Robert Fisher

[22]

Maggia

Ah!
Here she comes!
Reach for cover.
Her wicked eyes shine in the dark.
The glow-worm's light shows her evil face,
Her ugly face!
Three bats hide under her cloak.
She rides in a fiery chariot.
Snakes for reins!
Rats for horses,
With locusts as weapons,
She rides through the night.

Janice Cudmore (aged 9)

The Old Woman of Riddles

Once an old woman along the way
Fixed me with a beady stare,
And pointing her bony finger at me
Spoke – as I stood trembling there –

'Riddle me, riddle me, what is that
Over your head and under your hat?'

'What is it trembles with each breath of air,
And yet it can the heaviest loads bear?'

'I went to town and who went with me,
He whistled and moaned
But no one could see him.
Who was he?'

'I have a little sister, she lives near the ditch,
If you dare to touch her she'll give you the itch.'

'You can't guess this riddle
Within two hours,
It's a food you will find
That is full of flowers!'

'What is tall and thin, red within,
Nail on top, and there it is!'
(She said pointing)

'Riddle me, riddle me, riddle-me-ree,
What is that nutcracker up a tree?'

I looked up to where she was pointing,
And when I looked back she was gone,
Leaving one last question hanging in the air –
Did an old woman along the way
Fix me with her beady stare
And point her bony finger at me
And speak in riddles, as I stood there?

Robert Fisher

Answers:
hair, water, wind, stinging nettle,
honey, finger, squirrel

The Two Witches

O, sixteen hundred and ninety one,
Never was year so well begun,
Backsy-forsy and inside-out,
The best of all years to ballad about.

On the first fine day of January
I ran to my sweetheart Margery
And tossed her over the roof so far
That down she fell like a shooting star.

But when we two had frolicked and kissed
She clapped her fingers about my wrist
And tossed me over the chimney stack,
And danced on me till my bones did crack.

Then, when she had laboured to easy my pain,
We sat by the stile of Robin's Lane,
She in a hare and I in a toad
And puffed at the clouds till merry they glowed.

We spelled our loves until close of day.
I wished her good-night and walked away,
But she put out a tongue that was long and red
And swallowed me down like a crumb of bread.

Robert Graves

The Hag

The Hag is astride,
This night for to ride;
The Devil and she together:
Through thick, and through thin,
Now out, and then in,
Though ne'er so foul be the weather.

A thorn or a burr
She takes for a spur:
With a lash of a bramble she rides now
Through brakes and through briars
O'er ditches and mires,
She follows the Spirit that guides now.

No beast, for his food,
Dares now range the wood;
But hushed in his lair he lies lurking:
While mischiefs, by these,
On land and on seas,
At noon of night are a-working.

The storm will arise,
And trouble the skies;
This night, and more for the wonder
The ghost from the tomb
Affrighted shall come
Called out by the clap of the thunder.

Robert Herrick

Charm

Bring the holy crust of bread,
Lay it underneath the head;
It's a certain charm to keep
Hags away, while children sleep.

Robert Herrick

A Moon-witch

A moon-witch is no joke.
She comes as a sort of smoke.
She wisps in through the keyhole and feels
    about
Like a spider's arm or a smoke-elephant's snout
Till she finds her victim.
He collapses like a balloon – she has sucked him
Empty in a flash. Her misty feeler
Blooms red as blood in water, then milkily
    paler –
And fades. And a hundred miles off
She disguises her burp with a laugh.

Also she has a sort of electronic
Rocket-homing trick – and that is chronic.
She steals the signature
Of whoever she wants to bewitch
And swallows it. Now wherever he might be
He sees her face, horrible with evil glee,
Hurtling at him like a rocket – WHOP!
People see him stop.

He staggers, he smooths his brow, he is
    astonished –
Whatever it was, it seems to have vanished.

He doesn't know what he's in for.
He's done for.
Only deep in sleep he dreams and groans
A pack of hyenas are fighting over his bones.

In a week, he dies. Then 'Goodness!' the witch
    says,
And yawns and falls asleep for about ten days
Like a huge serpent that just ate
Something its own weight.

Ted Hughes

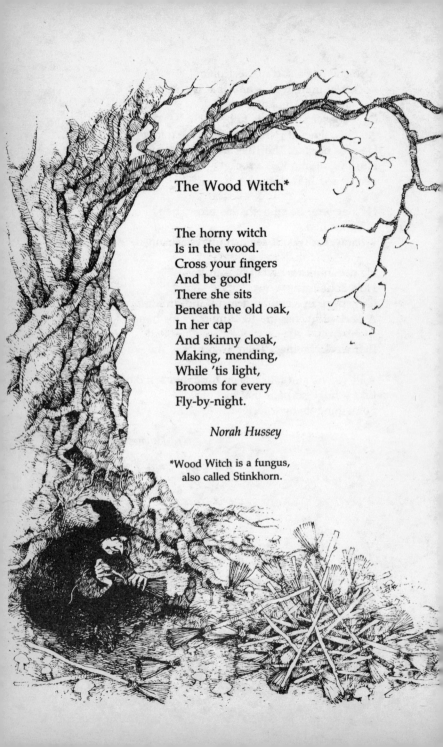

The Wood Witch*

The horny witch
Is in the wood.
Cross your fingers
And be good!
There she sits
Beneath the old oak,
In her cap
And skinny cloak,
Making, mending,
While 'tis light,
Brooms for every
Fly-by-night.

Norah Hussey

*Wood Witch is a fungus,
also called Stinkhorn.

A Witch's Charm

The owl is abroad, the bat and the toad,
  And so is the cat-a-mountain;
The ant and the mole sit both in a hole,
  And frog peeps out o' the fountain.
The dogs they do bay, and the timbrels play
  The spindle is now a-turning;
The moon it is red, and the stars are fled,
  But all the sky is a-burning.

Ben Jonson

The Witches' Song

'I last night lay all alone
On the ground, to hear the mandrake groan,
And plucked him up, though he grew full low,
And, as I had done, the cock did crow.'

'And I ha' been plucking (plants among)
Hemlock, henbane, adder's-tongue,
Night-shade, moon-wort, libbard's bane;
And twice by the dogs was like to be ta'en.'

'Yes: I have brought to help your vows,
Hornèd poppy, cypress boughs.
The fig-tree wild, that grows on tombs,
And juice that from the larch tree comes,
The basilisk's blood, and the viper's skin;
And now our orgies let's begin.'

Ben Jonson

The Egg-shell

The wind took off with the sunset –
The fog came up with the tide,
When the Witch of the North took an Egg-shell
With a little Blue Devil inside.
'Sink,' she said, 'or swim,' she said,
'It's all you will get from me.
And that is the finish of *him*!' she said,
And the Egg-Shell went to sea.

The wind fell dead with the midnight –
The fog shut down like a sheet,
When the Witch of the North heard the Egg-shell
Feeling by hand for a fleet.
'Get!' she said, 'or you're gone,' she said,
But the little Blue Devil said 'No!'
'The sights are just coming on,' he said,
And he let the Whitehead go.

The wind got up with the morning –
The fog blew off with the rain,
When the Witch of the North saw the Egg-shell
And the little Blue Devil again.
'Did you swim?' she said. 'Did you sink?' she said,
And the little Blue Devil replied:
'For myself I swam, but I *think*,' he said,
'There's somebody sinking outside.'

Rudyard Kipling

Charm Against an Egg-boat

You must break the shell to bits, for fear
The witches should make it a boat, my dear:
For over the sea, away from home,
Far by night the witches roam.

Anon

An old superstition says that when a boiled egg has been eaten, the bottom of the shell should at once be broken. This was to prevent witches from using the unbroken shell as a boat to sail the sea and brew up storms.

Hallowe'en

Witch's fiddle, turnip middle,
Scoop it all out with a spoon.
Curve mouth and eyes
With a careful knife
Beneath a Hallowe'en moon.

Witch-broom handle, long wax candle,
Stick spell-firm in the hole.
Find a match,
Step back and watch
Hushed as a Hallowe'en mole.

Witch-keen sight, strike bright light,
Match to the greasy wick.
See faint flame
Flick and falter,
Rise and stutter.
Part of the Hallowe'en game.

Witch-black cat; put turnip hat
Gently back on the top.
Turn out all moon.
Watch yellow eyes, mouth's flamed rays.
Hark for a Hallowe'en tune.

> For the witch's fiddle
> And the witch's cat
> And the crack
> Of a witch-broom handle
> Sing a haggard song
> On a moonless night
> To a turnip lantern candle.

John Kitching

Hallowe'en

'Granny, I saw a witch go by,
I saw two, I saw three!
I heard their skirts go swish, swish, swish –'

   'Child, 'twas leaves against the sky,
   And the autumn wind in the tree.'

'Granny, broomsticks they bestrode,
Their hats were black as tar,
And buckles twinkled on their shoes –'

   'You saw but shadows on the road,
   The sparkle of a star.'

'Granny, all their heels were red,
Their cats were big as sheep.
I heard a bat say to an owl –'

   'Child, you must go straight to bed,
   'Tis time you were asleep.'

'Granny, I saw men in green,
Their eyes shone fiery red,
Their heads were yellow pumpkins –'

   'Now you've told me what you've seen,
   WILL you go to bed?'

'Granny?'

　'Well?'

'Don't you believe –?'

　'What?'

'What I've seen?
Don't you know it's Hallowe'en?'

　　　　Marie A. Lawson

Witch Nastee Spella's Arrival
in Hangman's Wood

The clock struck
ONE.
Would Nastee Spella soon arrive?

The clock struck
TWO.
Would we all leave this wood . . . alive?

The clock struck
THREE.
Here she comes! Her broomstick's smoking!

The clock struck
FOUR.
She's fat as butter, no joking.

The clock struck
FIVE.
Her skin . . . a ghastly shade of green.

The clock struck
SIX.
Those piggy eyes, so sly and mean.

The clock struck
SEVEN.
Her cloak in tatters, hair like weed.

The clock struck
EIGHT.
That warty chin huge as a swede.

The clock struck
NINE.
In her pockets squirmed nests of rats.

The clock struck
TEN.
And gliding beside her were red-eyed bats.

The clock struck
ELEVEN.
'She's landing now!' yelled Wizard Good.

The clock struck
MIDNIGHT
As Nastee crashed into Hangman's Wood!

Wes Magee

Witch Nastee Spella's
Hallowe'en Stew

While Nastee stirred
   her black cat purred
and the cauldron popped and bubbled.
   The vile, blue stew
   looked thick as glue;
the poor guests' tummies were troubled.

She flung in ants
   and underpants
and holly shaped in a wreath,
   one cob of corn,
   a stifled yawn,
then her set of blackened false teeth.

She threw in keys
   and knobbly knees
plus a bottle of Worcester sauce;
   some rancid frog,
   a TV prog,
and one hair from a cowboy's horse.

Thick was the smoke
   (it made you choke)
but the Witch was pleased with her brew.
   She plopped in figs,
   innards of pigs,
cast spells for her Hallowe'en stew.

'You rotten lot,
    taste from the pot
or I'll turn you into white mice!'
    The guests dipped in
    (one imp *slipped* in)
and agreed it was . . . 'rather nice'.

    That dreadful scene
    turned some guests green,
and all so loud and so rude.
    Everyone burped
    and belched and slurped
as they guzzled the party food.

Wes Magee

Space Traveller

There was a witch, hump-backed and hooded,
    Lived by herself in a burnt-out tree.
When storm winds shrieked and the moon was buried
    And the dark of the forest was black as black,
    She rose in the air like a rocket at sea,
        Riding the wind,
        Riding the night,
    Riding the tempest to the moon and back.

James Nimmo

Green Magic

'Abracadabra – ABC':
There's magic in this apple tree.

I touch its bark, sing 'DEF':
Here's music that will wake the deaf!

I wave a branch, sing 'GHI':
My body feels the urge to fly,

Sing 'JKL' – and at the sound
I grow so light, I'm off the ground.

Then, as I murmur 'MNO'
The blossoms fall, the apples grow.

Intoning 'PQR' I pick
An apple – and it makes me sick!

I quickly gabble 'STU',
And see this sort of trick won't do:

It's 'V' – and I come down to earth;
'WX': what's magic worth? –

But, as I sing 'YZ', I see
There's magic here that's meant for me.

Edward Lowbury

Recipe

If I tell you this tale you might wince,
It concerns an odd mixture for mince,
Made from dogs' teeth and tails
By a witch from North Wales
In a pot with a pattern of chintz.
You take pigs' ears and lemons and cheese,
And the wings and the stings from queen bees,
Some frogs live and frisky,
A cupful of whisky,
Some slugs and a few black-eyed peas.
Boil it an hour or two,
Season with essence of shrew;
If it turns out too salty,
The frogs must be faulty –
There's nothing at all you can do
(Except throw out the whole beastly brew!)

Shelagh McGee

Frogday

I met a witch on Wednesday,
And Crabtree was her name;
I saw her next on Friday
And called her that again.
'Look here,' she said – her voice was bleak –
'We witches often change.
On Tuesdays I'm called Fenugreek,
On Thursdays simply Mange,
And if on Mondays you should call,
You'll find my name is Lizard;
On Sundays I've no name at all,
On Saturdays I'm Wizard.
But Friday is a witch's own,
The witchiest day of all –
I'm Magpie and I'm Megaphone,
I'm Grimsdyke and I'm Gall;
And when I'm feeling really bad
I'm Bogey, Boot and Blog.
Now if you forget all that, my lad –
You'll turn into a frog!'

Shelagh McGee

A Witch's Song

Now I'm furnished for the flight,
Now I go, now I fly,
Malkin my sweet spirit and I.
Oh, what a dainty pleasure it is
To ride in the air
When the moon shines fair,
And sing and dance and toy and kiss.
Over woods, high rocks and mountains,
Over seas, our mistress's fountains,
Over steeples, towers, and turrets,
We fly by night, among troops of spirits.
No ring of bells to our ears sounds,
No howls of wolves, no yelp of hounds.
No, not the noise of water's breach,
Or cannon's throat can our height reach.

Thomas Middleton

One Wild Witch

One witch wandered
the wild, wet wood,
Hubblum, Bubblum, Blum,
    cried she;
spilled her spells
from a deep, dark hood,
Rubblum, Troublum, Tree.

Two toads tripped
over thistles three,
Hoakum, Croakum, Crone;
found four frogs
by a chestnut tree,
Shoakum, Choakum, Groan.

Five fat finches
flew from their den,
Chirrupem, Cherrupem, Chee;
saw six snakes
and flew back again,
Stirrupem, Flirrupem, Flea.

Seven smart slow-worms
slid by a stone,
Writhem, Slithem, Slee;
eight eagles spotted them,
then there were none,
Spythem, Trythem, Tea!

Nine noisy nanny-goats
nibbled at the grass,
Nibblum, Dribblum, Dree;
never saw the witch
as she wandered past,
Whibblum, Whobblum, Whee.

Ten tall trees
heard the wild witch cry,
Hubblum, Bubblum, Blum,
   cried she;
waved her broom
then flew to the sky,
Rubblum, Troublum, Tree.

Slithery slow-worms,
nanny-goats, trees,
eagles, toads as well;
finches, frogs
and thistles three
flew off to the wild witch spell.

                    Judith Nicholls

Witch's Cat

is noiseless,
felt at dark
like silent breath;
stalker, not stalked,
a leaf or web
that brushes flesh,
the creak of empty stairs,
the cloud that darkens stars
and shrouds a moon.

Witch's cat
like fear, runs wild,
child of the shadows;
no child of light,
this silent cat of night.

Judith Nicholls

Let Us In

'Let us in! Let us in!'
Who is crying above the wind's din?

'Let us in! Let us in!
We are pale and cold and thin.'

A clock chimes the midnight hour.
Are they creatures with magic power?

'Let us in! Let us in!
We are pale and cold and thin.'

They come and come and more and more.
Close the curtains! Lock the door!

'Let us in! Let us in!
We are pale and cold and thin.'

'Let us in! Let us in!
We are pale and cold and thin.'

Olive Dove

The Alchemist

There's a mysterious light
Burns all through the night
In that house where some people say
The alchemist dwells
With books full of spells
And a cat who scares children away.

Some say that he lives
In that house all alone
Some say he has claws and a beak
Some say he keeps rats
And vampire bats
And a raven he's taught how to speak.

And the children play dare:
'I dare you to spy
Through the dust on his window pane.'
They say those who dare
To enter his lair
Have never been seen again.

They say that his furnace
Turns iron and bronze
Into ingots of glistening gold.
They say if you take
The powder he makes
You'll never fall sick or grow old.

Some say he's a wizard
Some say he's a saint
Some say he eats toads for his tea
So I don't think I'll pay
Him a visit today
For fear he should want to eat me.

Gareth Owen

Spell
(to be said to a balloon being blow up)

Love me, you'll grow fat and fly,
Hate me, you'll grown thin and die.
Sail, O sail the windy sky!
    Hate me, thinner,
    Nothing for dinner;
  Love me, fatter,
    Butter and batter.
Fatter, fatter, fatter, fatter –

BANG!

Ian Serraillier

Spell of Creation

Within the flower there lies a seed,
Within the seed there springs a tree,
Within the tree there spreads a wood.

In the wood there burns a fire,
And in the fire there melts a stone,
Within the stone a ring of iron.

Within the ring there lies an O
Within the O there looks an eye,
In the eye there swims a sea,

And in the sea reflected sky,
And in the sky there shines the sun,
Within the sun a bird of gold.

Within the bird there beats a heart,
And from the heart there flows a song,
And in the song there sings a word.

In the word there speaks a world,
A word of joy, a world of grief,
From joy and grief there springs my love.

Oh love, my love, there springs a world,
And on the world there shines a sun
And in the sun there burns a fire,

Within the fire consumes my heart
And in my heart there beats a bird,
And in the bird there wakes an eye,

Within the eye, earth, sea and sky,
Earth, sky and sea within an O
Lie like the seed within the flower.

Kathleen Raine

Mixed Brews

There once was a witch
Who lived in a ditch
And brewed her brews in the hedges.
She gathered some dank
From the deepest bank
And some from around the edges.

She practised her charms
By waving her arms
And muttering words and curses;
And every spell
Would have worked out well
If she hadn't mixed the verses.

Not long since,
When she wanted a Prince
To wake the Sleeping Beauty,
A man appeared
With a long grey beard,
Too old to report for duty!

When she hoped to save
Aladdin's cave
From his uncle cruel and cranky,
She concocted a spell
That somehow fell
Not on him but on Widow Twankey.

With a magic bean
She called for a Queen
Who was locked in the wizard's castle.
There came an old hag
With a postman's bag
And threepence to pay on the parcel.

What *comes* of a witch
Who has hitch after hitch?
I'm afraid that there's no telling:
But I think, as a rule,
She returns to school
And tries to improve her spelling.

Clive Sansom

Spells

I dance and dance without any feet –
This is the spell of the ripening wheat.

With never a tongue I've a tale to tell –
This is the meadow-grasses' spell.

I give you health without any fee –
This is the spell of the apple-tree.

I rhyme and riddle without any book –
This is the spell of the bubbling brook.

Without any legs I run for ever –
This is the spell of the mighty river.

I fall for ever and not at all –
This is the spell of the waterfall.

Without a voice I roar aloud –
This is the spell of the thunder-cloud.

No button or seam has my white coat –
This is the spell of the leaping goat.

I can cheat strangers with never a word –
This is the spell of the cuckoo-bird.

We have tongues in plenty but speak no names –
This is the spell of the fiery flames.

The creaking door has a spell to riddle –
I play a tune without any fiddle.

James Reeves

The Witches' Call

Come, witches, come, on your hithering brooms!
The moorland is dark and still –
Over church and the churchyard tombs
To the oakwood under the hill.
Come through the mist and wandering cloud,
Fly with the crescent moon;
Come where the witches and warlocks crowd,
Come soon . . . soon!

Leave your room with its shadowy cat,
Your cauldron over the hearth;
Seize your cloak and pointed hat,
Come by the witches' path.
Float from the earth like a rising bird,
Stream through the darkening air,
Come at the sound of our secret word,
Come to the witches' lair!

Clive Sansom

Riddle

What a hideous crackling and whistling
Interrupt my sleep!
I open the curtains. What do I see and hear? . . .
Two brooms brushing the tree-tops,
Two cloaks blowing in the wind,
Two cats holding tight,
Two jockeys shouting,
'I'll beat you to the moon! I'll beat you to the moon!'

I wonder *which* will win.

Ian Serraillier

Answer: two witches

The Spell of a Witch

I am making a magic spell,
With a toad and a goblin's yell.
A phantom's scream, a dragon's feather,
It smells as good as good as ever.
With frog's toes and lizard's legs,
I think I'll add some rotten eggs.
I scream and shout I moan and yell,
I've just found a snail's shell.
I'll add a pinch of dirty weather,
With a poison dragon's feather.
I stir my brew, I stir my brew,
Some for me and some for you.
Spooky, spooky dark and damp,
I met a wizard I met a tramp.
The wizard gave me a puppy dog's tail,
The tramp gave me a toad and a snail.
I stir my brew, I stir my brew,
Some for me and some for you.
I'll add some poison I'll add some blood,
I think it smells rather good.

Gillian Parker (aged 9)

The Witch's Cat

'My magic is dead,' said the witch. 'I'm astounded
That people can fly to the moon and around it.
It used to be mine and the cat's till they found it.
My broomstick is draughty, I snivel with cold
As I ride to the stars. I'm painfully old,
　　And so is my cat;
　　But planet-and-space-ship,
　　Rocket or race-ship
　Never shall part me from that.'

She wrote an advertisement, 'Witch in a fix
Willing to part with the whole bag of tricks,
Going cheap at the price at eighteen and six.'
But no one was ready to empty his coffers
For out-of-date rubbish. There weren't any offers –
　　Except for the cat.
　　'But planet-and-space-ship,
　　Rocket or race-ship
　Never shall part me from that.'

The tears trickled fast, not a sentence she spoke
As she stamped on her broom and the brittle stick broke,
And she dumped in a dustbin her hat and her cloak,
Then clean disappeared, leaving no prints;
And no one at all has set eyes on her since
　　Or her tired old cat.
　　'But planet-and-space-ship,
　　Rocket or race-ship
　Never shall part me from that.'

Ian Serraillier

The Witches' Spell

Double, double, toil and trouble;
Fire burn, and cauldron bubble.
Fillet of a fenny snake
In the cauldron boil and bake;
Eye of newt, and toe of frog,
Wool of bat, and tongue of dog,
Adder's fork, and blind-worm's sting,
Lizard's leg and owlet's wing,
For a charm of powerful trouble,
Like a hell-broth, boil and bubble.
Double, double, toil and trouble;
Fire burn, and cauldron bubble.

William Shakespeare

Prayer for a Night Safe from Ghosts, Sprites and Witches

Let no lamenting cries, nor doleful tears
Be heard all night within, nor yet without;
Nor let false whispers, breeding hidden fears,
Break gentle sleep with misconceived doubt.
Let no deluding dreams, nor dreadful sights,
Make sudden sad affrights;
Nor let house-fires, nor lightning's helpless harms,
Nor let the Puck, nor other evil sprites,
Nor let mischievous witches with their charms,
Nor let hobgoblins, names whose sense we see not,
Fray us with things that be not.
Let not the screech-owl nor the stork be heard,
Nor the night raven that still deadly yells;
Nor damned ghosts, called up with mighty spells,
Nor grisly vultures, make us once affeared;
Nor let unpleasant choir of frogs still croaking
Make us to wish their choking.
Let none of these their dreary accents sing:
Nor let the woods them answer, nor their echoes ring.

Edmund Spenser

(from *Epithalamion*, a poem to celebrate his wedding)

The Turn of the Road

I was playing with my hoop along the road
Just where the bushes are, when, suddenly,
I heard a shout. – I ran away and stowed
Myself beneath a bush, and watched to see
What made the noise, and then, around the bend,
A woman came.

She was old.
She was wrinkle-faced. She had big teeth. – The end
Of her red shawl caught on a bush and rolled
Right off her and her fair fell down. – Her face
Was white, and awful, and her eyes looked sick,
And she was talking queer.

'O God of Grace!'
Said she, *'Where is the child?'* And flew back quick
The way she came, and screamed, and shook her hands!
. . . Maybe she was a witch from foreign lands.

James Stephens

Hallowe'en
A Poem for Bedtime

What went bump in the pitch-black doorway?
  A wild-eyed ghost in chains and mail.
Did you hear a tap on the moonlit window?
  A terrible witch's fingernail.
Wasn't that a rattle in the far dark corner?
  Only a skeleton chattering its jaws.
Something is breathing in the unlocked wardrobe.
  A black woolly monster with long white claws.

They've all come to catch you
And scratch you at midnight,
To fight you and bite you,
  You can't get away!

Out of the mirror fly legions of demons!
  They're armed with pitchforks and want a game.
Can you smell burning, like roast pork and sulphur?
  Just a dragon, breathing flame.
What is that whispering, down on the carpet?
  Hundreds of goblins advance like a tide.
What are those shadows that move on the curtains?
  The banshees and werewolves grow restless outside.

They've all come to catch you
And scratch you at midnight,
To fight you and bite you
  And take you away!

Alan Temperley

Beware

Across the moon
Like veins of black
The dead tree's
Branches show.
Against the bark
Shadowed by cowl
She stands with
Eyes aglow.
'Tis her night tonight my friends.
Keep windows locked and barred.
'Tis Hallowe'en
'Tis Hallowe'en.
'Neath moon and cloud
In moaning wind
She moves
And
Aaaaaaahhhh--------

Joe Wood

The Witch's Work Song

Two spoons of sherry
Three ounces of yeast,
Half a pound of unicorn,
And God bless the feast.
Shake them in the collander,
Bang them to a chop,
Simmer slightly, snip up nicely,
Jump, skip, hop.
Knit one, knot one, purl two together,
Pip one and pop one and pluck the secret feather.

Baste in a mod. oven.
God bless our coven.
Tra-la-la!
Three toads in a jar.
Te-he-he!
Put in the frog's knee.
Peep out of the lace curtain.
There goes the Toplady girl, she's up to no good
                                        that's certain.

Oh, what a lovely baby!
How nice it would go with gravy.
Pinch the salt,
Turn the malt
With a hey-nonny-nonny and I don't mean maybe.

T. H. White

Curing Song

Your heart is good.
(The Spirit) Shining Darkness will be here.
You think only of sad unpleasant things,
You are to think of goodness.
Lie down and sleep here.
Shining darkness will join us.
You think of this goodness in your dream.
Goodness will be given to you,
I will speak for it, and it will come to pass.
It will happen here,
I will ask for your good,
It will happen as I sit by you,
It will be done as I sit here in this place.

Yuma Indians, North America

Index of Authors

Index of First Lines